A CLIMB THROUGH ALTERED LANDSCAPES

A Climb Through Altered Landscapes

Ian Parks

First Published in United Kingdom in 1998
by
Blackwater Press
PO Box 5115, Leicester LE2 8ZD

Printed in England by
Rural Press
Leicester, LE4 5JT

All rights reserved. No part of this publication may be reproduced in any material form (including photocopying or storing it in any medium by electronic means and whether or not transiently or incidentally to some other use of this publication) without the written permission of the copyright owner except in accordance with the provisions of the Copyright, Designs and Patents Act 1988 or under the terms of a licence issued by the Copyright Licensing Agency Ltd, 90 Tottenham Court Road, London, England W1P 9HE. Applications for the copyright owner's written permission to reproduce any part of this publication should be addressed to the publisher.

© Ian Parks 1998

Ian Parks asserts his right to be identified as the author of this work in accordance with the Copyright, Designs and Patents Act 1988.

Cover illustration by Daniella Westbrook

British Library Cataloguing in Publication Data
Parks, Ian
   A climb through altered landscapes
   I. Title
   821.9'14

ISBN 0 9528557 3 9

ACKNOWLEDGEMENTS

Bete Noire, Cascando, The Chiron Review (USA), *Contraflow, English* (Journal of the English Association), *Envoi, Footnotes* (Schools Poetry Association), *Foolscap, Giant Steps, Inkshed, New Voices in British Poetry* (California University Anthology), *The New Welsh Review, Odyssey, Orbis, Other Poetry, Outposts, Oxford English, Oxford Magazine, Oxford Poetry, PEN New Poetry II* (Arts Council Anthology), *Poetry and Audience, Poetry Nottingham, Poetry Review, Poetry Wales, The Poet's Voice, Quartz, The Reater, The Red Deer Anthology 2, The Rialto, Staple, The Wide Skirt, The Word.*

A Dream of Snow was broadcast on Poetry Now (BBC Radio 3)

Unicorns won the *Cascando* Travel Writing Prize in 1995

The Pearl was commissioned by the Posterngate Gallery in Hull.

Three poems were included in a pamphlet collection published by Littlewood in 1985.

The author would like to thank Yorkshire and Humberside Arts for an Award in 1985 and Hawthornden Castle for a Fellowship in 1991 during which some of these poems were written.

Blackwater Press gratefully acknowledges financial assistance from The National Lottery through The Arts Council of England.

for Karen

Contents

A Dream of Snow	11
Wintering	12
Snowbound	13
Unicorns	14
A Process of Selection	15
The Pearl	16
Hammock	17
Facing South	18
The Ridge	19
Epithalamion	20
From a Provincial Town	21
Strange Promise	22
Somersby	23
Departures and Rendezvous	24
Last Days	25
Castlerigg	26
Victoria Road	27
Overnight	28
The Girl from West Virginia	29
I'll Light a Candle for You	30
A Window to the West	31
Tiger Lilies	32
Lace	33
Towton	34
The Blizzard	35
Winter City	36
Urban Graveyard	37
The Beggars of Oxford	38
Anastasia	39
Life Mask	40
The Disinterment	41
The Old Age of Shelley	42
Nero and Agrippina	43
Emily	44
The Shore Near Viareggio	45
Atlantic House	46
Sea-Glass	47
Swimming in the Black Sea	48
The Lighthouse	49
Sirens	50

A DREAM OF SNOW

I woke to find our room
was open to the stars.
During that night the snow had come,
drifting through spaces where rafters
should have been. The tiles had slid
off silently to shatter on the ground.
Familiar things were hid:
I knew my slippers by the mound
of snowflakes there;
the mirror by its struggle to reflect
untrod carpet and frosted chair.
The clock I could detect
by a regular, muffled tick.
Quilted, I knew, was inadequate.
And though the snow lay thick
we were neither cold nor wet.
I tried to wake you then
to tell of what I'd seen
but was unable. When I spoke
words were frozen into crystals
on the quiet air. I'd left the wardrobe open:
in a queue behind the door
the stiffened shapes of our former lives
were waiting for the thaw.

WINTERING

The cottage settles back
into itself: a stillness
that was there before I came.
I trail my bedclothes
to the windowledge and sit
and wait. A sculpted valley
curving out of sight
with fresh snow lading every branch.
On my first night I heard
the distant drift; a soft
commencement which became
the killing avalanche.
Elsewhere, your hands
are touching down on objects
made familiar by desire -
candle, earring, paperweight;
yesterday's letter sealed
but still unsent. I breathe
against the glass and print your name.

SNOWBOUND

Like something wished for
but not quite fulfilled
this sudden snowfall
takes us by surprise.

All day I've held
your head between my hands,
brushed back the black
curls from your face,

smoothed out the sheet
and kissed your eyes.
Only the ridge, its crop
of trees distinct

against the white, has made
the middle-distance real.
Grateful for the smallness
of our home - the close

proximity of window, stove,
and bed - we let the steady hours
take their course. Making love
has always been like this:

a searching after
something undefined
in rooms where darkness
gathers to a blur.

But what is there to say
about the snow? It comes
upon us softly, flake
on flake, silently drifting

to our bodies' shape
then leaves us
as it found us, unawares:
raw, uncertain, half-awake.

UNICORNS

Sarajevo morning. I woke
on the fringes of the bombed-out town,
asking for water, rubbing my eyes.

There were others in the convoy
like myself - crashed in the back
of a transit-van among dismantled toys

and crates of Aid. Dawn broke
over a skyline gone for good:
wrecked statues, toppled spires,

the silence of a sniper
taking aim. The girl who shared
my sleeping-bag rolled over

on her side. Twenty hours
behind the wheel, hugging the Adriatic
all the way, she'd glimpsed them

in the corner of her eye,
down at the river, stooped to drink,
their whorled horns crossing

and their silver manes
dipped to the water, lost in mist.
A blurred heraldic tableau

overtaken by the check-point soldier
asking for ID. If anyone
could see them children would,

but the kids we saw were too far gone
to notice anything, except the fall
of European dust that settled

in the hospital. I missed my epiphany.
But somewhere back along the road
I sensed their hot breath rising

and their lowered horns.
I was distracted, disengaged;
looking too hard or not hard enough.

A PROCESS OF SELECTION

Once, in another country,
when I was reckless twenty
thinking it was love,
I slammed my glass down hard
and walked away. The sea

was as I'd left it -
silent, calm; and the peopled
island where I'd walked
reared like a dark mound
in the bay. That gesture marked the end

of what had almost not begun.
But things are different now.
The near sea still retains
its clear mid-winter glow
and I've abandoned any hope

of staying for much longer on this shore
where mussel-shells that crack
under my tread can show
their shades of willow-pattern blue.
It seems that love recurs

outside the common sphere
of what we say and what we are,
reducing me to silences like these
in which I make a choice between
the sharp edge and the smooth.

A process of selection, nothing more,
that finds me absent-minded here:
a figure out of season, out of reach,
caught between the high tide and the low,
stooping to the beach and skimming stones.

THE PEARL

Paint me as I am. It is enough.
My mistress will be satisfied.
Instruct me and I'll cast aside
doublet, hose and ruff,
exhibiting a nakedness she knows.

Let no dark shadow come between
the truth of what your eye has seen
and what you represent;
no intervening vine
or cloth of gold. The tapestry

will serve her purpose well:
a chase in which the quarry
is transformed. So paint me
as you'd paint a girl;
choose which parts to show

and which to hide. Make no addition
except this: hang her picture
from a further wall where she
may gaze forever on her prize
and from my earlobe drop a lucent pearl.

HAMMOCK

I spent that summer
slung between two trees,
waiting for the real life
to begin. Behind my eyes
the movement of clouds;
across the park small cries
diminishing. I was a part
of everything I saw:
the leaves shut tight
above me; the butterfly
that settled on my wrist.
What it was like
to throw away my teens,
swaying to the rhythm
of the day in sleeveless shirt
and cut-down jeans,
a six-pack cooling in the lake.
Afloat on a sea
of my own dreams, I was content
to let the pages fall
while Sonny Boy was blowing
sweet and low. I woke
to a sunburst splintering
the trees: a rush of light.

FACING SOUTH

Stairs lead to darkness
and to love: an unmade bed,
a rocking chair; whatever else
you choose to leave behind.

I gauge the spread
of sunlight through these rooms;
know how it brims
each surface and each plane

as gradual as a thought
fills out the mind.
Love needs a high room
facing south; a view

of rooftops, empty sky.
It takes place somewhere,
nowhere, here: the shape you make,
the space you occupy.

THE RIDGE

It was a bitter season -
cold, transitional. Whenever I looked up
I saw the ridge. It seemed
to level closer with each day.
Leaving wasn't easy
nor is this: the climb through altered landscapes,
different trees, to find
each other as we really are.
A black dog followed us
into the wood; a pair of lovers
looked the other way,
and we were left alone to dance
absurdly where the blossom fell. Only the moon
was constant, and one star.

EPITHALAMION

That this flat on the edge of town
overlooking a few yellow fields of ripe corn
is the best that we can do
matters very little to me. Strangely,
it matters even less to you,

brought up among similar fields,
the nearest bus route miles away.
Our wedding this hot summer
has meant you've had to leave
a prim cottage bedroom and a view

of lanes, hills, one prominent folly;
a remnant of the park's red deer
that still come close to graze.
It's all contracted to the limits
of these temporary rooms

we're sure to outgrow. Suddenly
late the other night *I'll take you home again Kathleen*
a passing drunk was bawling at our window
to where your heart will feel no pain.
It stirred up in me some vague feeling

I couldn't give voice to until now,
watching you dust from the windowsill
the gritty black husks of a hundred minute lives:
corn flies from the fields that in death
are like so many iron-filings everywhere.

Instantly I recall the first day in that cottage
you'd grown up in - a photograph
of you on the sideboard, given pride of place.
Behind the glass, freckling
your infant face and dotted in your hair

tiny corn flies from fields nearby.
Perfectly preserved in the corners
of the tarnished gilded frame
they'd found a way in years ago
and never could escape.

FROM A PROVINCIAL TOWN

These days, every letter I begin
makes oblique reference to its origin.
We visited our friends or *we stayed in*

seem forms of resignation at a time
when youth is on our side and home
is miles from any city. Then the questions come:

What can life elsewhere offer more than this?
Wet rooftops, fields fragrant after rain
and the promise of our common lot that is
the unexpected death, the odd familiar kiss.

STRANGE PROMISE

I always come back to this:
an overgrown bench in a garden
full of weeds that every stone path
leads me to. It is early morning

in my dream, and I am haunted
by a sense of guilt that stops me in my tracks
on the damp lawn. I stand
there for a while, listening to the rooks,

and waiting for some movement
at my side. It never comes.
But there is always the strange promise
of a touch, and the stranger

promise of a hand to hold.
My heart is overgrown. If it comes
to speaking I will speak.
If it comes to kisses I will kiss

SOMERSBY

I see a drenched September,
the sunk lanes leading nowhere
and the churchyard overgrown;
Tennyson and Rosa on their last

illicit walk. I have the final scene
by heart: a bitter conversation,
tears, regrets, somewhere the river
running through it all; the implications

of a young man's pain. A sadness
brooded over us all day,
as if the high-walled garden
and the birthplace weren't enough

to shift our focus for a while
and make the future plain. We,
or what will be the ghosts of us,
will tread these paths again.

DEPARTURES AND RENDEZVOUS

It had to end like this: with rain
and muted headlights streaming through
the station porticoes. We kissed
and in my haste I left the map,
its edges curling to pale tints.
A futile gesture after all -
absurd and half-deliberate,
hoping at last you'd chance on it
when you cleared out the back. All our
departures and our rendezvous
as clear as when we saw them first:
the cities flat in their grey sprawl
and spa-towns smudged with fingerprints.

LAST DAYS

They have a movement of their own,
these last days spent with you
in our high room. A week of rain
and the graveyard's overgrown,

hoarding its nest of greenery;
while over there, through open blinds,
the wasteground too is waterlogged.
They're sinking the foundations

of the new development, but time
is against them, progress is slow.
Fold back the sheets, step from your dress;
slow down the movement of these days

to the pulse of lovers after sex.
The fire-escape rusts orange
in the rain; and here you're pausing,
waiting for a sign. I came for nothing less.

CASTLERIGG

When I discovered that the time was right
I pitched my bed among the standing stones.
It was the perfect place for making love:

a huge moon rising where the shadows fell
and all the landscape gathered round to look.
The sky was flooded where we slept -

the colour of a bloodstain, spilt red wine.
Our dream was interrupted with a cry.
Next morning when they found you in my arms,

I had no word to offer except this:
the circle was inviting, set apart.
We live under its shadowline.

VICTORIA ROAD

It was there you said you felt
the first tentative flutter of new life,
catching your breath as you caught your eye
reflected in the antique shop glass.
I think of us perfected there
and how I was infatuated by
that string of amber beads
roped loose about your neck,
each glowing round distended
at the point of birth.

The mirror holds us still,
among the post-imperial bric-a-brac -
your hand in mine; the other hand encompassing
what was engendered there.
This is where we take our bearings from:
the cluttered grandeur
of a faded age: cracked china cups
with gold edged round the rim,
frail christening robes of the long dead;
great drops of Whitby jet.

OVERNIGHT

For weeks they slept together in the heart
of the frozen city. Down in the street
the troops limped past on ice. Statues
were shattered in the public squares;

voices fell silent in the afternoons.
For the first time now they slept apart:
from his high attic room with the fractured pane
he squinted at the far grey quarter

where she lay awake, turning her dark
familiar head under pale domes and spires.
At the station, when he stooped to kiss
goodbye, she found the button of his uniform

and slipped a hand inside his shirt.
Next morning they woke up to find
the wires were down, the barriers manned,
and all love's interchange cut short.

THE GIRL FROM WEST VIRGINIA

I met her on a Greyhound
heading south, still smarting
from the decades of defeat.
We shared a can of Miller
and she smiled. Her snake-belt buckle
showed in bold relief
the high tide of the Civil War -
a thin grey line at Gettysburg;
the southern army going down
in fields of harvest wheat -
and under it, in Rebel red and blue,
The South Will Rise Again.
Snow veered across the windscreen.
Drugstores and graveyards
broke the white; Old Glory
frozen on a pole. Her red-check shirt,
her careless smile, she reminded me of you.
New England is a Greyhound
heading south, and the girl
from West Virginia coming through.

I'LL LIGHT A CANDLE FOR YOU

Midnight and the darkness
coming down; I light a candle
to your memory and place it

where I know it will be seen.
My room fronts on the avenue:
if you drive past you'll see it,

if you don't it burns there
nonetheless - a fleeting agent
glimpsed through sheets of glass

with imperfection flawing
every grain. This late
in the day you won't detect

what moves behind it or what
makes it move in this high room
where something might begin.

Only, from the streets, it lights
your given name. It draws you
to the window; pulls you in.

A WINDOW TO THE WEST

What more should love require of us
except we house together
on this unpeopled headland
where tides are treacherous?
To walk from here - a point
where lovers made a pact
and stepped into the sea -
is treacherous indeed.
And what more should we ask?
I could outlive my usefulness,
surviving in the shadow of a risk
not taken. The place is fixed:
a stacked unpointed tower
with a window to the west
through which we'd gaze,
a pale sea-haunted couple
married, almost, to each other
and certainly to this:
a cold, clear-calling morning,
salt sharpening our need,
and the heart at high tide
in its chamber beating.

TIGER LILIES

Did you get back to find them
starved of air, unopened
in the hot room where we danced?

I held you and you wore
your velvet dress: black, absorbent,
swallowing the light.

Or were they open-throated
when you came, turned to the window
where you used to sit -

self-centred, self-contained -
distilling their potential
as the moon burned fierce and red?

All night their fragrance
promised something more: a scent
too like the scent of death

suspended in the air;
the crude Byzantine crucifix
I nailed above our bed.

LACE

What I expected when you promised lace
was some plain token worked in your own hand -
collar, belt or handkerchief - not this:
a bodice nipped and tightened at the waist
and your dark body under it.
Later, draped across a cane-work chair,
all it contained of you was scent.

You left it there for me to find
next morning as I shaved.
In factories all over town
well-oiled machines were making it come true;
but I could think of nothing but your hands
patiently looping through the afternoon
a fabric meshed and perfect.

TOWTON

You at the roadside,
the wind in your hair,
and nearer than you know
the shallow graves

of those who died
by the thousand here
in a cause you wouldn't
think worthwhile.

I could have told you how
the stream ran blood
for miles, and how the killing
didn't stop until it grew

too dark to tell
the living from the dead.
Perhaps I did, although
the memory is lost.

I can't believe
a battle fought in snow
one bleak Palm Sunday
five centuries ago

should make you stop your car
beside the gritty monument
unless, by being there,
you re-enact my argument:

that the past is a process
through which we must suffer.
But you at the roadside
with the wind in your hair,

you've lived long enough to know
it has no solutions to offer.
I used to think it did.
And that is where we differ.

THE BLIZZARD

Sometimes there are four of us
and sometimes there are five

if what the captain says he sees
is true: an unknown other

gliding through the storm
and we bent double, tethered

to a line. And though he says
we haven't lost our way

I know his compass lies.
It leads us back and back again

to that same widening
ravine - pure, sheer-sided,

crystalline - we left before
the avalanche crashed down.

And now I need to sleep.
Who is it kneels beside you

as you try to lift your head,
spreading your shoulders

with a net of gold? She whispers
what you knew and then forgot.

So trust in darkness for a while:
the snow is warm, the ice is hot.

WINTER CITY

Lost in the city of your choice
I followed clues of accident and rhyme.
Streets led down to a tidal river,

rotting hulks, the Customs House,
a rail-bridge curving over
which I crossed. Then nothing

but the shifting coastal flats
where things dissolve their likeness
into mist. I saw it from above -

a map of squares and alleyways,
floodlit statues, stone arcades;
the high room where you sleep alone -

and wondered where my heart
might lead me next, at one
with its long history, its slow pain.

Winter condemned the city at a stroke.
In quayside bars the music stopped;
the singers kissed each other and went home.

I was decided, wrapped around;
leaving on the night train south
to find a city of my own.

URBAN GRAVEYARD

I dreamt it once
and now the dream survives
in hints and shadows,
corners of the eye -

or in an urban graveyard
hemmed around with houses
and a red-brick factory
where snow persists

and ice delineates
the features of
such long-forgotten lives
as bring us here with camera and with pen

to chart a landscape
no-one knows exists.
Is this where Hardy's lovers met
when urns were still unfallen

and the lettering was new
to press chaste palms
and share a holy kiss,
as if imagination were enough

to animate the angels
from their plinths? There are
no answers here for you
and so we turn to go,

stopped in our unmelted tracks
by icons of a secret sisterhood:
sunk headstones, unchained gates,
and all the dead of Jericho.

THE BEGGARS OF OXFORD

You might not want to hear
about the girl who stopped me
in my tracks the other night
but I might want to tell you
nonetheless. Before I knew it,
it was dark. Like someone
in a frozen frame, her face lit
by the street-lamp's glare,
she leaned out from the shadows
easily. Begging was perfected
in her smile, her outstretched arm,
the shortness of her dress.
And when she spoke she didn't speak
to me but to some other
breathing on my neck. A stranger
in the city, I escaped
down alleyways I knew I would forget.
Take in the blackbird
and the wounded hare; such cold
raw creatures in distress.
Small coins changed hands. I ran
across the square. Our limit,
like our need, is bottomless.

ANASTASIA

Your namesake survived the bullet and the blade;
crossed continents of ice and fire
to fool a generation with her smile.
I see you waltzing underneath the stars,

your slender body poised before the fall;
the Winter Palace silent under snow.
I met you at the terminus years after the event;
you wore your hair as she did -

taut and coiled. And though you're always there
my Russian girl, skating the frozen river
of my dreams, time's intricate perspective
breaks the glass. A shutter clicks

and fixes you in an unguarded moment,
as you were in Moscow or St. Petersburg:
a captive princess wrapped in furs
with hailstones melting in your hair.

LIFE MASK

You knew the death mask well enough.
And so did I: the poet dead
at twenty-six, a plaster gag
stretched tight across the lips;
cold flesh under a colder sheen.

Then why should this be different?
Black on black, each eyelash
fine, distinct; the face serene
and months from death. How was it done?
There must have been a moment

of suspended disbelief;
presentiments, however vague,
of the choking time that's still to come:
smoothed forehead, eyelids closed,
a holding back of breath.

THE DISINTERMENT

We came with torches
in the middle of the night
to lift the coffin-lid

and peer inside. A moth flew out,
powdered our faces
with its wings and settled

in the architrave. His lordship
claimed the darkness
undisturbed - a coronet,

a signet-ring, a velvet cushion
pillowing the head. Someone
ran their fingers through his hair,

snipped off a keepsake,
prised an eyelid up. We noted
all the details in our book,

examined with great care
the cloven foot; measured
his penis, declared it false.

Do not forget the sneer
that curled his lip, or how
the heart was buried somewhere else.

THE OLD AGE OF SHELLEY

Some bright and dying creature
passed this way, his face half-hidden,
disguising every feature
but his wild and fatal eyes.

What is there in our nature
makes us fear the beautiful,
the dissident, the free;
renouncing changes
in our lives for a future
beggared, laced with compromise?

Enquire of me. All afternoon
he sits and sips his wine,
accosting strangers with a tale
of fiery youth - elopement, encounter,
mind-searing verses, suicide;
a chance escape from death by water
and since then not a line.

NERO AND AGRIPPINA

He kneels to take his mother
by the arm; she draws him to her face.
It comes so close to being a crime
he quivers where he lies
as if the past and future were
embedded in that slow embrace.

Are we, too, victims
in an accident of time
that we should weep to watch them
as they kiss? Look long and hard:

she holds him and she lets him go -
a naked, lithe and ruined boy
who soon will put her to the sword.

EMILY

Seven nights of dreaming. On the last
she came in silence to my bed -
prim, uncertain - dressed in white,
and white from her long sojourn
with the dead. I didn't dare to touch her

or to speak, though she spoke
gently, from that high reserve
in fits and starts and dashes
like her poems; a searing whiteness
cancelling out all I'd written,

all I'd said, until one image
shimmered through the rest:
my great-grandmother as I saw her once,
before she welcomed death in and began
her long withdrawal into radiance.

THE SHORE NEAR VIAREGGIO

The beautiful cripple
strips to his waist;
too near the blackened limbs
of his drowned friend.
A place like nowhere else
on earth: smoke rising
from the makeshift pyre;
incense drifting bitter-sweet

among the stunted trees.
Each stroke removes him
from that windless shore -
its brackish shallows
pierced with reeds;
the days together
and the years apart.
His breath comes slow

in this thin air
who swam the Hellespont.
That night he dreams
of angels, their wing-tips
overlapping, touching down,
searing the rim
of our inconstant sphere.
One plucks at something

in the flames;
another rakes the ashes,
burns his hand. Go back
sometimes to Viareggio,
make supplication
to the gods of the place
and in a cask of wine
preserve the heart.

ATLANTIC HOUSE

Here, on the western seaboard,
things affirm their close affinity
with light. A haunted cottage
at the water's edge, where night
after night you slept with me,

our room a landlocked cabin -
closed, confined - and all
our acts of love took place
within earshot of the sea.
So much was unexplained:

tread the floorboards, you could hear
the creak of timbers overhead,
rigging cast a shadow on the wall,
a strange hook twisted down
above the bed. We tilted

on the sand-bank easily.
The sun sank early, making room
for those who'd gone before
like us to watch its furious light
dispersing iridescence in the bay.

We learned a new vocabulary
of compass, log-book, chart;
a beach of stones and shingle
stretched away. I loved you,
so I let the tide begin

its slow erosion into nothingness.
Under the beams, our ghosts
are kissing still. I see
you on the shore in your white dress,
turning as you did after the dance

and take with me the salt taste
of your eyes; a smooth grey pebble
for a paperweight. When all else fails
I haul my sheets onto the ledge
and let the wind fill out my sails.

SEA-GLASS

By the time you're old enough to understand
what passed between us on that shore
the essence of its moment will be lost;
but how could I forget
the cold and rawness of that day
or how the sea-glass caught your eye

among dead crabs and mussel-shells?
It was as if the coastline of the north
had shrunk its length around we three -
a man, a woman and a child,
out for the day in winter clothes.
At first we didn't notice how the sand

gave way to shingle then to glass;
a narrow strip we almost crossed
without considering its worth.
I lifted each transparency
to the clear mid-winter light,
not knowing or not caring if the tide

would wash them into grains of nothingness,
handing the fragments back
for you to keep. Nothing was spoken;
no lessons had been learned.
Only the sea kept up its endless noise.
Mistaken for a family

we climbed back through the town -
its shops, its pubs, its alleyways
intrusive in the bitter afternoon -
leaving behind us on the shore
a trace of footprints intercrossed
and silences where things were overturned.

SWIMMING IN THE BLACK SEA

The bracelet I gave you:
nothing else. You go down
to the water's edge each morning
as the sun begins to rise

on new republics coming free
of dust. That is how
I saw you when I woke -
your body white under the waves,

the Black Sea bleaching
each blue bead to grey
all through the tedious weeks
of your exchange -

and this is how such images persist.
Not here, not now, but in
another here and now
you take a dive and surface

in the centre of this poem,
your black hair dripping salt
onto the page; the bracelet
I gave you on your wrist.

THE LIGHTHOUSE

Think back: remember the lighthouse
poised on the windswept head;
or rather the approach to it -

a long road unwinding through acres
of dark pasturage and fields of gorse,
affording glimpses of its vivid beams,

distinct at first but losing their identity,
criss-crossing over miles of open sea.
This is what it's like to be in love:

to find perspectives shifting constantly;
to always be approaching some fixed point
but never arriving at its source.

SIRENS

It was the morning of the second day.
We came down from the eastern ridge
as mist was clearing from the fells.
Scree fell sheer into the lake. At first
we thought their singing was the sound

of ice-wind wailing through the man-shaped rocks,
then someone pointed and we gazed
wide-eyed into the deepening blue
as if a child had cast a stone
and we were waiting on the edge

to catch its endless, soundless fall
through glacial waters to the bed;
expecting nothing as the bubbles broke
on silence and a silver thread
we followed till it came to rest.

She surfaced near us on a rock -
sleek, bare-breasted - holding in her arms
a mirror, shells, freshwater pearls.
We waded deep to hear her sing.
She turned green eyes upon us, stopped our hearts,

transfixed us with the sureness of her voice.
Her flesh was our flesh for a while;
a cold and embraceable thing.
I think we saw the faces of our wives
as we first knew them in the glowing dawn,

before we grew accustomed to the light.
Her sisters were identical, their scaled backs
arching, dripping liquid glass,
returning to their element
as we returned to ours. Nothing is the same.

We feed and sleep like creatures without choice.
Raising our simple crosses, we belong.
Something has passed that will not come again.
We heard strange music, waterfalls;
our end in the beginning of their song.